OLD LEADHILLS

JOHN FYFE ANDERSON

The large building towards the right of this view, set back from Main Street, is Leadhills Primary School. It was opened in November 1903. The previous school was located beside the Miners' Library. It had been in poor condition and had received adverse comment from teachers, parents and education inspectors. In June 1902 a summary of the H.M. Inspector's report on the old school stated the following: 'The school is conducted with care and ability and makes on the whole a good appearance. Provincialisms abound in reading, and while words are correctly named, there is want of modulation and expression in reading and repetition. Explanation of passages read and repeated should receive greatly increased attention. Composition is not more than fair and geography of III and IV should be taught on a more intelligent system. In other respects, results in standard and class work were satisfactory. A start is to be made in the erection of new premises.' The headmaster of the new school in 1903 was James McFarlane who was in charge of four teachers and 120 pupils. The school leaving age at that time was fourteen.

Text © John Fyfe Anderson, 2012.
First published in the United Kingdom, 2012,
by Stenlake Publishing Ltd.
54–58 Mill Square, Catrine,
Ayrshire, KA5 6RD.
Telephone: 01290 551122
www.stenlake.co.uk

ISBN 9781840335828

**The publishers regret that they cannot supply
copies of any pictures featured in this book.**

ACKNOWLEDGEMENTS

Thanks to Mike Davis, Mrs Mary Hamilton, Ken Ledger and Alex F. Young.

The publishers wish to thank Leadhills Miners' Library for permission to reproduce the photographs on pages 28, 44 (right), 45, 46 and 47 from its collection.

BIBLIOGRAPHY

Cameron, M. and Harvey, W.S., *Leadhills Library* (pamphlet) n.d.
Harvey, W.S., *Lead and Labour, The Miners of Leadhills* (website).
Ireland, A., *The Leadhills and Wanlockhead Light Railway*, Kelso, 1990.
Kaufman, P., *Leadhills: Library of Diggers*, n.d.
Le Harivel, J.P., *Leadhills Study for Clydesdale District Council*, 1989.
New Statistical Account, Parish of Crawford, 1835.
Third Statistical Account, Leadhills, Parish of Crawford, 1953.
Files of the *Hamilton Advertiser*.

INTRODUCTION

Leadhills is the second highest village in Scotland and is located at a height of 1,295 feet above sea level. It is in South Lanarkshire, five and three-quarter miles west south-west of Elvanfoot near the source of Glengonnar Water. Leadhills, along with nearby Wanlockhead, had the most important lead ore deposit in Scotland.

Lead mining has taken place in the area since the thirteenth century. However, it is possible that the Romans extracted lead from these parts in the first and second centuries. Little was known about the ores until the early sixteenth century and it was not until the seventeenth century that lead mining began to be developed on a large scale. Gold was also found in the Lowther Hills and in the sixteenth and seventeenth centuries a number of persons obtained patents in order to search for precious metals.

Records of mining operations in the area only date from about 1600. During the seventeenth century Sir James Hope of Hopetoun acquired the lands of Leadhills as a result of his marriage to Anna, daughter and heiress of Robert Foulis of Leadhills, a goldsmith in Edinburgh. Sir James devoted much attention to mining operations there.

By the 1790s great quantities of lead were being found in Leadhills and it was fetching a much higher price than ten years previously. The mines at that time were being managed by the Scotch Mining Company who employed 200 men. These included pickmen, smelters, labourers and also washers who were often boys. In addition, there were carpenters and smiths. The owner of the mines by this time was James, third Earl of Hopetoun, and as rent he received every sixth bar of lead produced. In 1810 the mines at Leadhills produced about 1,400 tons of lead but for some years afterwards the annual output was reduced to between 700 and 800 tons. From 1842 the ores of Leadhills were extracted with the assistance of steam power and improved smelting facilities.

By 1860 all of the Leadhills mines were operated by the Leadhills Mining Company. This company invested in a reservoir and also new machinery. From this period the miners used dynamite in their operations. Lead ore was being mined 780 feet below sea level by 1868. There was an underground railway that extended to a length of two and a half miles. In addition, there were four water wheels and two hydraulic engines.

In 1878 the Leadhills Mining Company surrendered its lease to a syndicate who established the Leadhills Silver Lead Mining and Smelting Company. A further change occurred in 1903 when the Leadhills Company commenced mining operations and continued with the lease until 1929. In 1931 the Leadhills Company was reformed and became a limited company. This company sold road stone and also mined lead ore but ceased trading in 1938. The remainder of the plant was sold at auction in 1940.

Most of the remains of mining activity that can be seen around Leadhills date back to the most active period of lead mining from the late eighteenth century to the early nineteenth century. To the north of the village there is a great gash in the hillside known as Lady Manner's Scar where the Susanna Vein is located. It produced more lead ore than any other vein in the area.

The miners of Leadhills had access to a library which was founded in 1741 and was known as the Leadhills Miners' Reading Society. The miners at that period had relatively short working hours and could take advantage of reading a wide range of literature in the library. The original library building still stands in Main Street. The Rev. Thomas Anderson, writing in 1835, referred to the Miners' Library in the following description: 'The terms of admission and annual subscription are extremely moderate and consequently afford every facility for intellectual instruction, this in some measure accounting for the character which the workmen have long had of possessing a more than usual share of intelligence for men in their situation.'

The population of Leadhills has declined over the centuries. In the mid-eighteenth century it was more than 1,400 but by 1791 it had declined to 1,118. There was a further reduction by 1861 when the figure was 896. By 1953 the population was 650 and the most recent figure is 315.

The poet Allan Ramsay is one of the village's famous sons, along with William Symington, pioneer of steam navigation. Famous visitors to the village include the poet William Wordsworth and his sister Dorothy who came in 1803. They were accompanied by another poet, Samuel Taylor Coleridge, and Dorothy recorded the visit to Leadhills in her *Recollections of a Tour Made in Scotland*. In 1769 Thomas Pennant, an early travel writer, came to the village on his first tour or Scotland.

The Rev. J.C. Lough, who wrote the entry for Leadhills in the *Third Statistical Account* in 1953, concluded his contribution on an optimistic note when he stated the following: 'What can be said with assurance is that however much the world lying beyond the hills may change, these same hills have a constant influence on the people here, an influence that cannot change and which makes for uprightness of character, independence of thought and a rugged individuality that cannot but be admired. With such qualities informing the village today we can safely leave the future to look after itself, knowing that the people of Leadhills will face it with courage and calm whatever it brings.'

Leadhills had a very important role in the lead-mining industry in Scotland and generations of miners laboured there for centuries. The village occupies a position of some significance in the industrial history of the nation and it was designated as a Conservation Area in 1989. This designation continues to protect and enhance the character and unique identity of the village.

Leadhills

The rural location of Leadhills is shown to advantage in this view. The grouse moors surrounding the village amount to more than 11,000 acres and are considered to be amongst the best in Scotland. Many centuries ago the glens and hills surrounding Leadhills were described as 'God's Treasure House in Scotland' because of the rich deposits of minerals which were being mined underground. At one time, there was a house on the outskirts of the village where free overnight accommodation was available to any beggar or pedlar who had undertaken the ascent to it. The design of the majority of the houses in this community derives from the basic miner's one storey cottage. Some of these cottages have been extended vertically to form one and a half or two storey houses.

With its linear nature in which the blocks of houses form the streets, the distinctive townscapes of Leadhills and nearby Wanlockhead are unique in Scotland. The streets are generally laid out from north to south along the contours of the valley. Some houses were built into the hillside where there were suitable sites and many of them were built on rock ledges. The majority of properties had no garden at the front with the streets running directly outside. However, there is front garden ground across the track or road from the houses in parts of Main Street, Ramsay Road, Lowther View and Symington Street. Smoke can be seen coming from the chimneys of the properties in this scene. Peat was used at one time for domestic heating and later coal was brought from the village of Douglas.

Lowther Hills and Hass Cottage, Leadhills.

The Lowther Hills were a stronghold of the Covenanters who were supporters of the National Covenant of 1638. First signed in Edinburgh, the covenant's purpose was to oppose the new forms of worship in the Church of Scotland which had been proposed by King Charles I. Covenanting ministers who were against the introduction of bishops and the appointment of ministers chosen by landowners were deprived of their parishes. As a result, they began to organise religious services outdoors, these being known as conventicles. There were various skirmishes between Covenanters and government forces in the Lowther Hills. As well as lead, gold was also found in the area; the crowns of King James V and his bride, Anne of Denmark, contained gold from the 'Leade-Hilles'. In 1951 Queen Elizabeth the Queen Mother was given a brooch which contained some gold from mines in Leadhills and gold from the area is also contained in the mace for the new Scottish Parliament which was re-established in 1999.

Leadhills from the Golf Course

Situated on moorland at 1,500 feet above sea level, Leadhills Golf Course is the highest course in Scotland and the second highest in Britain. The highest is the West Monmouthshire Golf Club in South Wales where the fourteenth tee is located at 1,518 feet above sea level. The village's nine-hole course is somewhat of a challenge because of the high winds that can be experienced due to its altitude. There are wonderful views to be obtained from over the entire course, the best being from the eighth tee. Leadhills Golf Club was founded in 1881 and was originally known as Lowther Golf Club.

A photograph of the bowling green in the village, taken in the summer of 1933. On 2 September of that year the bowlers of Leadhills had as their guests three rinks from Blackwood Bowling Club. Leadhills won the game by 20 shots. A press report stated: 'The visitors were entertained to tea purveyed in the Boarding House in most capable fashion by Miss Paton.' Mr Nimmo, secretary of the Blackwood Club, stated that both he and the club members were delighted 'to visit the heather hills in such lovely sunshine and meet their old friends.' The president of the Leadhills Bowling Club in reply extended a welcome to the Blackwood Club members and expressed a desire that their annual encounters would continue in the future.

The Curfew Bell occupies a prominent site in the village square and was built by the Scots Mining Company in 1770. Its purpose was to call miners to work and children to school. The bell was also rung when there were accidents in the mine, at funerals, and when people were lost on the hills. Its sole use now is at Hogmanay when it is rung to welcome the New Year. In this view from 1927 the bell has four timbers on its base; now there is a rough cast concrete plinth. It is thought that the Curfew Bell was built to commemorate James Stirling (1692–1770), a former mine manager whose reforms had a major impact on the community. He saved the mines from financial ruin when he came to Leadhills in 1734 and introduced many changes in the miners' lives by reducing their daily hours of work from twelve to six, raising wages, building houses with gardens and establishing a health insurance scheme. He also arranged for a doctor to be in the village and improved the educational provision for children in the local school. It was James Stirling who had the idea of a people's library, which became a reality when the Miners' Library was founded. He was known as 'The Venetian' because he had lived in Venice for ten years during which time he had tried to discover the secrets of the glassmakers in that city.

Farquhar Munro, a retired gamekeeper reads the notice board in the village on a sunny day sometime in the early decades of the twentieth century. The Curfew Bell can also be seen here along with the rows of miners' cottages. The residents of these cottages were great readers as a result of access to the large selection of books available in the Miners' Library. By the early 1950s the younger people preferred to go the cinema, dance halls and football matches which meant that it was necessary to travel out of Leadhills. Older residents played golf and bowls, fished, indulged in gardening and attended concerts on rare occasions. At an earlier period the Rev. J.C. Lough stated that the women of the village 'engaged in knitting and sewing and darning, in attending prayer meetings and mothers' meetings, and in general, keeping the home going.'

This is a view of Leadhills North Church of Scotland and manse which formed one building and was located in Ramsay Road. These premises were demolished in 1938. The last minister of Leadhills North Church was the Rev. Robert Condie Hunter who demitted office in 1936, having served since 1923. In 1937 the North Church united with Leadhills South Church. The minister of the united congregation was the Rev. Thomas Lee Law who served from 1937 to 1943. He was succeeded by the Rev. Eugen Wilfred Rushworth who was minister from 1943 until 1951. In 1952 a further union took place between the Church of Scotland congregations in Leadhills and Wanlockhead and the united congregation was known as Wanlockhead and Leadhills Church. The first minister of this united congregation was the Rev. J.C. Lough who wrote the entry for Leadhills in the *Third Statistical Account* in 1953. The first minister of the parish of Leadhills was the Rev. Stewart Smith, appointed in 1867 when the parish was disjoined from Crawford. However, regular church services had begun in the village in 1738. The cost of maintaining them was undertaken by Charles Hope, first Earl of Hopetoun.

The building on the left in Ramsay Road is the Leadhills North Church of Scotland and manse, seen here in June 1933. Twenty years later the writer of the entry for the village in the *Third Statistical Account* stated that while only a few of the houses had a telephone, in order to facilitate local calls an automatic telephone exchange had been built in Ramsay Road on the site of the old parish church.

This church has been used by the village's Church of Scotland congregation since 1937. It was built in 1883 for members of the Free Church of Scotland which came into existence as a result of the Disruption of 1843 when there was a major split in the Church of Scotland over the issue of patronage. This was a system whereby the ministers of parishes were chosen by heritors (landowners) without members of the congregations having any say in the matter. It is thought that half of the membership of the Church of Scotland entered the Free Church. In 1900 there was a union between the Free Church of Scotland and the United Presbyterian Church, which resulted in the formation of the United Free Church of Scotland. The former Free Church became a United Free congregation and later a Church of Scotland congregation as a result of the union at national level between the U.F. Church and the Church of Scotland. The church is now known as Lowther Parish Church.

THE POST OFFICE AND BOARDING HOUSE, LEADHILLS

On the immediate left of this 1922 photograph is Leadhills Post Office in Main Street. At an earlier period, in the 1880s, Leadhills was described as having a post office under Abington, with money order, savings bank and telegraph departments. There were also many more postal deliveries in an age before e-mail and mobile phones. In the 1950s there were two postal deliveries in the village and three uplifts of mail on weekdays. The Boarding House is on the right of this view. Today it would be described as a guest house. Many people in former years, particularly from Glasgow, came to stay in Leadhills on holiday weekends. A press report of 8 April 1933 stated the following: 'The first Glasgow holiday of the year brought the usual influx of visitors to spend the weekend in the village . . . . The visitors have greatly enjoyed their sojourn and many gathered to wish them goodbye on Monday evening.'

The Miners' Library, built in 1741, was the first private subscription library in the United Kingdom. A record of membership of the library from 1743 until 1902 is still in existence and the total number of members over that period was 870. The library began with 23 founding members who signed the register on 15 April 1743. From 1881 the membership records include nineteen women. The conditions of membership were stated in 'Articles and Laws of the Leadhills Reading Society', which were first written in 1741 and amended in 1859. A potential member was required to write to the Preses (Chairman) and at the next quarterly meeting be admitted to membership or rejected. After payment of 15p a new member was presented with a certificate and also required to pay the annual fee of 10p. The Preses was elected at the annual meeting. Other office bearers were the Clerk, Treasurer, three Librarians, an Assistant Librarian and six Inspectors. Three of these Inspectors were obliged to be present at the meeting every month when books were exchanged and to 'estimate the damage done to Books by the Members'. In addition, they had the authority to visit members in their homes in order to inspect any books which had been loaned. Paul Kaufman has referred to the library in the following terms: 'What is important is its significant expression of this isolated community, first through the original collective impulse which inspired and mustered practical support for such a novel undertaking and then of course through persistence of the institution for these two and a quarter centuries.'

Beechwood, Leadhills.

Beechwood was a row of houses with a baker's shop, which was occupied by Thomas Bryce. He was listed as a baker at this address in the 1911 census but some years later the shop was taken over by the Leadhills Co-operative Society and is still remembered as the Co-op bakery. This shop has since been demolished.

The staff of the Leadhills Co-operative store pose for the photographer outside their premises in Ramsay Road. There are well-stocked window displays which also include two posters advertising a circus. In former times the annual gala days in the village were organised by the society. On the fourth annual gala day in August 1933 nearly all the children of the village and a large number of adults met outside the Co-op store. The children were in fancy dress, a press report commenting that this 'presented a most brilliant spectacle and bore evidence of great taste and originality in characterisation.' After some speeches there was a procession of about 200 children, led by the Douglas Water Prize Silver Band, which went round the village. Decorated motor vans displaying Co-op products also took part in the procession. The children followed the band to the Drill Hall where tea and cakes were provided. Afterwards a programme of children's sports was held. There were also various events for adults, including a high-kicking event for men and a race for old men!

The houses known as Sunnyside and Roselea. Both of these substantial properties were built by the brothers Thomas and Robert Marr in the early 1900s. Thomas lived in Sunnyside and Robert lived in Roselea. In the 1911 census Thomas Marr's occupation was given as a waterwheel keeper; Robert's was given as a timberman in the lead mines.

This part of Leadhills, Flexholm, was rarely photographed as much greater attention was given to other areas within the village. A man is seen walking along what is present-day Main Street in the direction of Wanlockhead.

A young boy stands near Main Street in this scene from the early twentieth century. The gable-end of the Hopetoun Arms Hotel can just be seen on the right. Main Street has the most diverse range of properties in the village with the simple basic cottage, the larger one and a half storey houses, and also those with two storeys. It has a higher quantity of non-standard house types and some 'public' and 'commercial' buildings. Towards the end of the nineteenth century many businesses were located in the village. There were two boot and shoe makers, a butcher, and nine grocers and general merchants which included one licensed grocer. Further businesses were two tailors and clothiers, one draper and clothier, and a joiner and wright. The proprietor of the Hopetoun Arms Hotel had a bakery business and was also a coal agent.

These miners' cottages on Backrow were formerly bereft of modern amenities. However, by the early 1950s most of them had electric power and a water supply. Apart from the lack of amenities in their homes, miners experienced health problems as a result of their working conditions. It is recorded that in 1953 former miners had chest problems because of lack of ventilation in the mines. Many also had heart disease, high blood pressure, arterial disease and rheumatism. Many miners died at a very young age and evidence of this can be seen in the local cemetery. These cottages were well built with thick walls as protection against the harsh climate. It was the men of Leadhills who built many of the cottages with their own hands and they also kept them in a good state of repair.

A variety of groups and individuals are recorded for posterity in this open prospect of Townfoot. A solitary workman with a spade on his shoulder can be seen on the extreme left while two other men are working in the foreground. A small group of men are standing beside the gable-end of the cottage on the left and there are also children to be seen. The horse and cart was a common sight at a time before the widespread use of motor vehicles. The long row of cottages are in the present Symington Street.

Two boys face the camera in this photograph taken at the top of Ramsay Road in 1909. A variety of architectural styles can be seen on this slope, which was originally known as Jock's Brae. Colin McWilliam wrote in 1975 with reference to the village that 'its vernacular logic defies the rules of orderly planning'. It was usual for Scottish mining villages to be isolated. However, none are more remote than Leadhills and Wanlockhead. In the early 1950s the Rev. J.C. Lough pointed out that the older people in Leadhills were often confined to their houses when there was snow and ice in the winter. He also drew attention to the weather when he stated: 'The village can be filled with mighty tearing winds that beat upon the ear, deafening every other sound.'

The Hopetoun Arms Hotel in a traffic free Main Street is on the left of this view from 1909. It was originally built in the mid nineteenth century as a hunting lodge for the Hopetoun Estate. In 1661, as a result of an Act of Parliament, local leadmines were granted to Sir James Hope of Hopetoun. He had been appointed as Governor of the Mint in 1641 and Lord of Session in 1649. His son, Sir Charles Hope was elevated to the peerage of Scotland in 1703 with the titles of Viscount Aithrie, Baron Hope and Earl of Hopetoun. From 1722 to 1742 he was a Representative Peer for Scotland in the House of Lords. John Adrian Louis Hope, seventh Earl of Hopetoun, was created Marquess of Linlithgow in 1902. In 1900 he had been appointed as the first Governor General of Australia but resigned after less than two years as he considered that his salary had not been set at a high enough level. The first marquess also served as Secretary of State for Scotland in 1905. His son, Victor Alexander John Hope, was Viceroy of India from 1936 until 1943.

Hotel and Main Street, Leadhills

There was formerly a photographer's studio in Main Street at the junction with Station Road. It was occupied by William Hunter Scott (1863–1918) who photographed Leadhills and its environs in the first decade of the twentieth century. He also took photographs of families and local groups in his studio. His residence in the village was Ashlea House at the bottom of the Vennel, and seen here on the right. In 1903 W.H. Scott was awarded second prize in a worldwide photographic competition which was held in London. His prize was £30, a considerable sum at that time. Scott had only taken up photography three or four years previously but had obviously gained much expertise. The subject of his winning entry was a girl who was the daughter of a shepherd in the Leadhills area and the work was entitled 'A Rustic Beauty'. Scott's studio later became a shop and subsequently was rebuilt to form two cottages. This well-known local photographer was buried in the village cemetery.

Ashlea House at the foot of the Vennel was also the childhood home of James Alexander who was born in the village in 1836. He later became the owner of J. Buchanan and Company, coach and motor car builders in Glasgow. He also served as a bailie of the city. James Alexander was interested in the welfare of the miners in Leadhills and their families. In 1892 he made arrangements for 40 tons of coal to be given to 'deserving families'. On his death in 1924 he left £134,430, an enormous sum at that time. A total of £100,000 was left to the County Council of Lanark. The wording of the bequest was as follows: 'The annual income thereof to be applied in providing suitable nursing and medical attendance, medicine, medical and surgical appliances and necessaries for invalids and convalescents among the inhabitants of the village of Leadhills.' There is a stained glass window in Lowther Parish Church which commemorates him.

The village's war memorial is located opposite the Hopetoun Arms Hotel in Main Street. The names of seventeen men who lost their lives during the First World War are inscribed on the memorial. They are: Thomas Neilson Blackwood; John Brown; James Cook; Thomas Dunlop; William Harkness; David Hope; David Moffat McLean; William Menzies; Adam Miller; Walter Miller; John Wilson Noble; William Park; William Paterson; John Simpson; Andrew Smellie; and Joseph Williams. Thirteen of the above men were born in Leadhills. Walter Miller was born in Edinburgh and William Park was a native of the village of Crawford or the parish of that name. Andrew Smellie was a native of Greenock. John Wilson Noble does not appear to have any family connections with Leadhills and his birthplace is unknown. The war memorial also includes the names of William Dempster and Thomas Harrison McLintock who lost their lives during the Second World War. William Dempster, an Able Seaman and native of the village, was buried in the local cemetery. Thomas McLintock was born in Lochmaben, Dumfriesshire, but has no known grave.

LEADHILLS WAR MEMORIAL

The Leadhills war memorial was unveiled on Sunday, 20 August 1922 by Mrs Stephen Mitchell. A report in the *Hamilton Advertiser* stated the following: 'The ceremony soul stirring in its simplicity, was the most touching and impressive which has ever been held in Leadhills and will occupy a permanent place in the annals of the village.' Almost a thousand people attended to remember the seventeen fallen men of the village. There was a great procession to the memorial, which was led by pipers followed by buglers. Following them were Major Stephen Mitchell, Mr. W.T. Hall, convenor of the War Memorial Committee, and the children of the village. Bringing up the rear of the procession were the massed choir and the Leadhills Silver Band. The procession also included ex-servicemen from Sanquhar, Crawfordjohn, Abington, Elvanfoot, Wanlockhead and Leadhills. Mr. W.T. Hall presided at the ceremony which began with the Leadhills Silver Band playing 'Dead March in Saul'. There then followed a short religious service in which local ministers, the Revs. John McGarrity and G.G. Ramage, took part. A tribute to the war dead of Leadhills was given by Major Mitchell after which wreaths were laid by relatives, ex-servicemen, children, members of the public, and the War Memorial Committee. Seventy-five men from Leadhills served in the armed forces during the First World War.

The rural position of Leadhills is seen to advantage in this view with the backdrop of the Lowther Hills. The Miners' Library is on the right while on the left the Boarding House advertises teas and refreshments. This photograph was taken in 1933 and shows a lorry which is likely to have completed the long ascent up to the village. There would have been little traffic at that time as very few people owned cars. There were regular train services from Leadhills Station although this closed in 1938 and was replaced by a bus service. The station has reopened in recent years.

Symington Place was named after William Symington, pioneer of steam navigation and one of the famous sons of Leadhills. The cottages here were situated under the monument to William Symington which can be seen on the hillside above them to the right, roughly behind the two storey house in the middle of Symington Place where William was born. The cottages in Symington View faced towards the monument. Both areas are now known as Symington Street. The cemetery on the far right contains the grave of John Taylor who is reputed to have died in 1770 at the age of 137. He came to Leadhills to work in the mines at the age of 95 in 1732 and retired in 1751. At the age of 116 he was fishing in the hills when he was caught in a blizzard and failed to return home. However, a search party found him alive.

The railway line to Leadhills was built in 1900 for the Caledonian Railway Company in order to transport refined lead to central Scotland. Its highest point was 1,498 feet above sea level. Caledonian wagons can be seen in this view. In the late 1930s work ceased in the lead mines but a passenger service on the railway continued to operate until the end of 1938. Many years later, in 1983, the Leadhills and Wanlockhead Railway Society was established and as a result a two feet gauge tourist railway was built between the villages on the old standard gauge trackbed. Track laying began in 1986 over the quarter-mile route and a new station was built at Leadhills. At the present time diesel locomotives are used but there are plans for using a restored steam locomotive. The signal box at Leadhills contains mechanical equipment from the West Highland Line and also terra cotta bricks from the demolished Risping Cleuch Viaduct, which was on the route of the original railway line.

Station staff and the crew of a steam engine, seen here at Leadhills Railway Station in the early years of the twentieth century. It was here that the railway line reached a height of 1,405 feet. For many centuries the lead mining companies in Leadhills had to rely on horses and carts to convey their goods. It was not until the middle of the nineteenth century that the Caledonian Railway had built a railway line over Beattock Summit when the line was being constructed from Glasgow to Carlisle. Shortly after this time the Glasgow & South Western Railway constructed a line which linked Kilmarnock and Dumfries. As a result Leadhills had access to a main line railway system which was only seven miles to the east and west. The main problem regarding a railway line to the village was its high location. A further obstacle in the late nineteenth century was that a railway line, not at excessive cost, was unable to be constructed in such a mountainous area and still conform with Board of Trade regulations. The situation did not alter until the Light Railways Act of 1896. The Caledonian Railway applied for a Light Railway Order on 19 January 1897, this being confirmed on 5 August 1898. A report in the *Hamilton Advertiser* on 28 November 1899 stated the following: 'Work has begun on the seven mile section from Elvanfoot to Leadhills: close on 100 men are employed and they create no small stir in the village on a Saturday night.'

In this view a freight train has just left Leadhills Station and is on its way to Wanlockhead. The two houses were lived in by railway staff, the house nearest the track being occupied by the station master at Leadhills and the other by the engine driver. In the foreground there is the road which led to Wilson's Shaft. By the mid 1890s the local communities in the Leadhills area were in contact with the Caledonian Railway Company regarding a rail link to the nearby main lines. It was their opinion that such a link would result in greater development of the lead mines and an increase in freight traffic in both directions. In addition, it was suggested that a railway would bring visitors to the area and thus benefit the local economy. The Light Railway Commission held a public enquiry on 14 April 1897. The seventh Earl of Jersey chaired this ten-man commission, which included the following representatives from the Caledonian Railway Company: James Thomson, general manager; Irvine Kemp, general superintendent; George Graham, chief engineer; and John F. McIntosh, locomotive superintendent. Mr. H.B. Neave, solicitor for the Caledonian, informed the members of the commission that no objections had been lodged against the building of a railway. He also stated that the seventh Earl of Hopetoun, the main landowner in the area, was willing to make the land for the railway available without charge.

This viaduct was the largest structure which was built on the light railway. It was situated just over four miles from Elvanfoot, at Risping Cleuch, and was officially listed as underbridge No. 38. The viaduct was built of concrete by Sir Robert McAlpine who had first used this material for the Glenfinnan Viaduct on the railway line from Fort William to Mallaig in 1901. Major Crutt of the Board of Trade was the railway inspector who examined the building of the viaduct and his report of 20 September 1901 describes it in the following terms: '158 yards in length with 8 square circular arches each of a 50ft. span and 80ft. at its extreme height. It appears to be standing well and possesses sufficient theoretical strength.' An article in the *Railway Magazine* of December 1901 described the viaduct as 'a most effective and ornamental structure'. Construction was completed in September 1900 and all of the 70 men who had assisted in the building were invited to a social in the Masonic Hall in Leadhills by Mr Thomas McAlpine Jnr.

An angler awaiting a catch stands on the banks of the River Elvan near the distinctive bridge with its two circular arches. This bridge, built of concrete, was located just over a mile from Elvanfoot and was demolished a few years ago. The front of a steam engine can be seen on the right of the picture. One problem on this railway line was the risk of lineside fires in hot dry weather which could spread to the heather on the hills alongside the track. The weather also caused problems in the winter. Shortly after the railway was in operation there was a report in the *Hamilton Advertiser* of 21 December 1901 which stated the following: 'The severity of the snow storm has caused a great deal of inconvenience in the district. On Saturday the light railway was blocked, the drifts in some places being six to ten feet deep. Although two powerful engines were attached to the snow plough along with a squad of about eighty men it was about four o'clock in the afternoon before clearance was effected.'

The platform area of Leadhills Station extended to 70 yards. A crane with a capacity of three tons was built in the siding area and a goods shed was later built which had a lean-to extension where the platform was located. The station buildings included the station master's office, a waiting room and a gentlemen's lavatory. The stations at Leadhills, Wanlockhead and Elvanfoot all had a telephone connection. Glengonnar Mine was located only half a mile from Leadhills Station; a small siding was built at the mine in 1907 and this remained until 1937. The train service from Elvanfoot to Leadhills began on 1 October 1901 and the first train had a large number of passengers including some officials of the Caledonian Railway. There was much excitement at Leadhills and large crowds waited at the station among whom were children who had been given an official school holiday. Later in the day these children went by train to Elvanfoot where they had lemonade and biscuits supplied by Mr Paton who was a local wine merchant.

A somewhat anxious looking boy is seen in this view of sheep shearing at Lowthers, Leadhills, taken in the early years of the twentieth century around the time of the opening of the Leadhills and Wanlockhead Light Railway. There were four large sheep farms on the side of the railway line between Leadhills and Elvanfoot but there was no fence alongside the railway and there were many sheep which crossed the line on a daily basis. A report in the *Hamilton Advertiser* in May 1902 stated the following: 'The sheep give considerable trouble to the engine driver Mr W. Orr. Mr Orr, however, is a very cautious and careful driver and is always on the alert and prepared to draw up whenever he observes sheep on the line. Since the opening of the railway in October last some four sheep have been killed, a very trifling number when it is taken into account that on the four farms there are some 90 score (1800) sheep.' This report also stated that Mr Orr's vigilance had been the means on many occasions of preventing accidents since the beginning of the lambing season.

Sheep dipping at Lowthers in 1905. Dipping became compulsory in the early twentieth century as a protection against parasites. Somewhat unusually in this scene there are three well-dressed women observing the process, which usually took place in July, shearing having taken place in June. In the early 1900s hand sheep shears were used by the shepherds. This was extremely hard work especially with a flock of hundreds of sheep. Hand shears are only used on a small scale nowadays although some hand shearing competitions still take place at agricultural shows.

Left: William Hunter Scott, the well known Leadhills photographer, also photographed local 'characters' in addition to village scenes and groups. 'Heather Jock' was a tramp who visited Leadhills every year in order to sell besom brooms which he had made out of heather. A besom can be seen at his feet and some heather is being held in his right hand. 'Heather Jock' lived in the border town of Hawick for forty years.

Above: 'Old Margaret' was another of William Hunter Scott's subjects. Her full name was Margaret Hislop and she worked in the Hopetoun Arms Hotel. She also performed menial tasks such as mucking out byres. Here, she is wearing a tartan shawl which was a common form of dress for women in the early 1900s.

Allan Ramsay is one of the famous sons of the village and was born there in 1686. His father was a mine manager. Ramsay was educated at the school in Crawford and in 1701 he went to Edinburgh where he became an apprentice to a wig maker. It was in the capital that he began to write poetry. He later became a bookseller, one of his shops being in the city's High Street where he founded what was probably Britain's first circulating library in 1725. Ramsay's premises became a meeting place for the literary personalities of the city. In 1720 a collected edition of his poems was published and two years later his *Fables and Tales* appeared. Further publications were *The Ever Green* in 1724, which was an anthology of Middle Scots verse, and *Tea-Table Miscellany* which appeared in five volumes between 1724 and 1737. His best known work is 'The Gentle Shepherd' of which Robert Burns was a great admirer. Ramsay died in 1758 and the site of his former house in Edinburgh is commemorated in the city's Ramsay Gardens. His son, also Allan Ramsay (1713–1784), became one of Britain's finest portrait painters.

ALLAN RAMSAY

.. POET ..

BORN AT LEADHILLS, OCTOBER 15TH, 1686

Published by W. G. PARK, LEADHILLS.

Top-hatted and smartly dressed outriders pose with the Prince of Wales's Team in 1903 beside the wall of the Hopetoun Arms Hotel. The Prince of Wales at that time was Prince George who was the only surviving son of King Edward VII, monarch from 1901 to 1910. After the death of his father Prince George became King George V and reigned from 1910 until 1936. Prince George married Princess Mary of Teck at St James's Palace, London, on 6 July 1893. As a commemoration of her wedding a ring of gold from the mines of Leadhills was presented to Princess Mary by William G. Barron, a former mine manager, and miners of the area. After their Coronation she became known as Queen Mary.

A brass band leads a procession up Main Street around 1934. Processions were a regular feature of village life and took place on gala days. A great procession to celebrate the Coronation of King Edward VII occurred on 26 June 1902, the original date for this event, which was delayed until 9 August the same year because of the king's illness. On that late June day a procession lined up in front of Leadhills Public School, including children, lead miners, workmen with tools, Foresters, Masons and the general public. The procession was led by the Douglas Colliery Brass Band. All of the children wore a Coronation medal while Coronation mugs with attached ribbons dangled at their necks. The procession went round the village and ended in the Volunteer Park where tea was served to over 700 people.

I.L.P. SCOUTS LEADHILLS DEMONSTRATION JUNE 4 1910

In 1909 the miners had a dispute with the Leadhills Company regarding the siting of machinery. After an attempt at negotiating with the management the miners made the decision to join together as a trade union. The Leadhills Company did not accept this situation and there was a lock-out which lasted for seven months, finally ending in June 1910. This meant that miners were unable to work during that period. On 4 June 1910 there was a demonstration in Leadhills which was organised by the Glasgow branch of the Independent Labour Party. There was a procession consisting of locked-out miners and Labour Party members from Glasgow and Motherwell. Villagers also took part and there were a number of bands in the procession. In the evening there was a mass meeting at which the estimated attendance was 5,000 people. Speeches were given by Mr R. Smillie, a former Labour party candidate, Mr James Kerr, Independent Labour Party organiser, and Mr David Cairns, secretary of the Lanarkshire Miners' Union. This dispute was finally settled on 7 June when the Leadhills Company withdrew the condition that trade union members could not be employed. However, the company required the miners to sign an agreement promising not to harass non-trade union members and the manager gave an assurance that he would be impartial with all workers. The agreement was accepted by both parties and a press report stated: 'Rejoicings in the village followed.'

Left: This photograph taken on a spring day in 1908 shows a group of young girls and adults from Leadhills United Free Church on their Sunday school trip. The banner being carried is that of 'Leadhills United Free Church Sabbath School'. The girls in the foreground are all smartly dressed and wearing hats but only one of them appears to have noticed the photographer!

THE MINES, LEADHILLS.

The Glengonnar Mine, which is now disused, at one time provided much employment for the men of Leadhills. Formerly there was a shaft that was as low as sea level which permitted extraction of ore from what was known as the Brow Vein. The shaft later collapsed and in 1903 the Leadhills Company commenced operations with the intention of reopening it. The company's consultant engineer, Captain Borlase, suggested that electric power should be installed below ground. Over 3,000 tons of ore were produced in a single year at the new mine. The Glengonnar Mine closed in 1929 and work was transferred to the Borlase or Wembley mine. It was the opinion of many mining engineers that if there had been further development at Glengonnar the mine could still have been maintained as a profitable business. The ruins of the old powerhouse can still be seen at the minehead.

This monument commemorates William Symington, a pioneer of steam navigation, who was born in Leadhills in 1761. He was the son of a mine superintendent and had originally intended to become a minister before embarking instead on his career as a civil engineer. His interest in steam engines began when he was working for the Wanlockhead Mining Company. Symington devised improvements to the steam engine for which he obtained a patent in 1787. He built his first mine engine in 1791. Symington was also interested in furthering the wider application of steam power and in 1786 he built a working model steam carriage but was unable to promote its commercial development due to lack of funds. A further significant development occurred in 1801 when he patented an engine which resulted in direct drive to the paddle wheels of boats. This engine was installed on the *Charlotte Dundas II* and there were successful steam trials in 1803 but his sponsors decided against future development of the engine. After this time Symington experienced financial difficulties and there was a reduction in the demand for his pumping and lifting engines. He experienced some unsuccessful business ventures in mine management and had problems because of expensive lawsuits. In declining health Symington went to live in London with his daughter in 1829, dying two years later. He made a major contribution to the development of steam navigation and he claimed to have been the first person in the United Kingdom 'to effectively apply the power of the steam engine to the propelling of vessels'.

Right: A varied group, possibly visitors to the village, stand beside the William Symington monument in this scene. The monument occupies a prominent position near the cemetery. It was financed by public subscription and was unveiled on 12 June 1891, sixty years after William Symington's death. The monument is made of granite and was produced by Mossman and Co., well known Glasgow sculptors. It is decorated with brass panels showing Symington in portrait form and also includes an image of the *Charlotte Dundas II*.

The height and climate of Leadhills can result in very severe weather conditions. The village lies in a valley which runs from north to south with few trees for shelter. It is also exposed to the full force of the prevailing south and westerly winds. The design of the houses in the village has been influenced by these conditions. This is a scene from the winter of 1963 with snow almost covering the houses in Main Street. The man in the centre is Douglas Cowell. At an earlier period, in the 1780s, it was recorded in the *Statistical Account* that a man from the Leadhills area froze solid in the snow. His body was not found until the following April. The account also mentioned that in June 1791 frost and a shower of hail were severe enough to freeze water to at least a quarter of an inch. As a result crops of potatoes and kale (a type of cabbage) were badly affected.

Miners and two young boys gather at the entrance to the library where they had access to a wide range of high quality reading material. In 1906 there was an attempt to attract younger readers and the books which were purchased at that time included *The Boys' Own Annual* and *The Girls' Own Annual*. The miners of Leadhills underwent various crises in the final years of mining operations. The Union of Gas Workers and General Labourers brought out some men on strike in 1916. The activities of this union were criticised by Robert Smillie, former President of the Miners' Federation of Great Britain. The Leadhills miners later rejoined the Lanarkshire Union of Mine Workers. In 1921 the Leadhills Company reduced wages and the miners went on strike. The Leadhills Company finally ceased mining operations in 1929.

A group of men, most likely miners, outside the Miners' Library. Among the books from which they chose their reading material was fiction, volumes of plays including Shakespeare, theological works, history and mineralogy. There were also works by classical authors such as Homer and works by Thomas Carlyle, John Ruskin, Henry Fielding, Jonathan Swift and Henry Wadsworth Longfellow. A large category in the library was described as miscellaneous, one title being *The Truth About Drink*. As a result of the success of the Miners' Library two nearby villages decided to form Reading Societies. Wanlockhead Reading Society was established in 1756 and that of Westerkirk in 1792.

The interior of the library. On the right is the pulpit type seat of the Preses (chairman) and in the centre of the ceiling is the trap door which led to the loft where the 'Mining Bargain Books' and the journals were kept. By 1821 there were 1,500 books in the library, increasing to 3,805 by 1904. Later acquisitions brought the total to 5,000 volumes. Dorothy Wordsworth, sister of the poet William Wordsworth, visited Leadhills in 1803 and made the following comment: 'We found that they had a large library . . . that Lord Hopetoun had subscribed liberally to it, and that gentlemen who came with him were in the habit of making larger or smaller donations.' This famous institution was closed in 1965 when a mobile library service was introduced. However, the people of Leadhills realised that they had lost a place of national importance and a village committee began a long campaign to restore the library. On 3 June 1972 the Miners' Library was reopened.

Townfoot Row, May 1908.